Youthful Spark
Youth Energizers, Activities and Games

(Igniting the Fun in Youth)

Gerard Assey

Youthful Spark
Youth Energizers, Activities and Games
Igniting the Fun in Youth
By
Gerard Assey
© Copyright 2024 by Author

Published by:
Gerard Assey
19/18, Palli Arasan Street
Anna Nagar East
Chennai - 600 102

ISBN: 978-81-971121-7-1

(Image courtesy Freepik: www.Freepik.com-Thank You)

Table of Contents

28.   Hot Potato
29.   Limbo
30.   Sock Puppet Theater
31.   Bingo
32.   Paper Bag Skits
33.   Duck Duck Goose
34.   DIY Bracelets
35.   Frisbee Tic-Tac-Toe
36.   Giant Jenga
37.   Blindfolded Obstacle Course
38.   Shadow Puppet Show
39.   Bucket Ball
40.   Guess Who?
41.   Cup Stacking
42.   Bean Bag Toss
43.   Human Tic-Tac-Toe
44.   Balloon Stomp
45.   Name That Tune
46.   Water Relay
47.   M&M's Icebreaker
48.   Mindful Minute
49.   Buddy Interviews
50.   Memory Game

Some Ice Breakers

1. Name Game
2. Two Truths and a Lie
3. Human Bingo
4. The Great Egg Drop
5. Group Juggle
6. Quick Draw
7. Would You Rather?
8. The Great Wind Blows
9. Story Starters
10. The Memory Jar

Energizers, Games, and Activities for Youth:
A Comprehensive Guide

Welcome to a world of fun, energy, and engagement! This book is designed to be your go-to resource for a wide range of energizers, games, and activities that will inspire and captivate the youth of today. Whether you're a teacher, youth group leader, camp counselor, or parent, you'll find plenty of ideas here to keep young minds active, bodies moving, and spirits high.

The Importance of These Energizers, Games, and Activities for the Youth of Today: In today's fast-paced world, young people are often faced with a myriad of challenges, from academic pressure to social media distractions. It's more important than ever to provide them with opportunities for fun, creativity, and physical activity. Energizers, games, and activities offer a break from the routine, a chance to unwind, and a platform for social interaction. They also promote valuable skills such as teamwork, problem-solving, and creativity, which are essential for success in the modern world.

How to Use This Book: This book is organized into sections based on the type of activity, making it easy to find the perfect game or energizer for any occasion. Each activity is described in detail, including the objective, age group, number of participants, materials required, setting, timing, how to conduct the activity, trainer observations, prompting discussion, and application/learning.

To get the most out of this book, consider the interests and preferences of the youth you are working with. Choose activities that are age-appropriate and align with your goals. Feel free to adapt and modify the activities to suit your needs and the needs of your group.

This book is not just a collection of games; it's a tool to help you create memorable experiences, build relationships, and make a positive impact on the lives of the youth you serve. So, dive in, get creative, and have fun!

The Role of Energizers, Games, and Activities in Personal & Professional Development

Energizers, games, and activities play a crucial role in personal and professional development by providing opportunities for growth and learning in a fun and engaging way. Here are some key ways in which these activities can contribute to personal and professional development:

- ✓ **Teamwork:** Many activities require participants to work together towards a common goal, fostering teamwork and collaboration skills. This is essential for success in both personal and professional settings.
- ✓ **Communication:** Activities that involve verbal and non-verbal communication help participants develop effective communication skills, which are essential in all aspects of life.
- ✓ **Problem-solving:** Games and activities often present challenges that require creative thinking and problem-solving skills to overcome. These experiences can help develop critical thinking skills that are valuable in both personal and professional contexts.
- ✓ **Leadership:** Some activities require participants to take on leadership roles, helping them develop leadership skills such as decision-making, delegation, and conflict resolution.
- ✓ **Emotional Intelligence:** Engaging in activities that evoke emotions can help participants

develop emotional intelligence, which is crucial for building strong relationships and managing stress.
- ✓ **Fun and Engagement:** Perhaps most importantly, these activities provide a fun and engaging way to learn and grow, making personal and professional development enjoyable and rewarding.

1. Balloon Pop Challenge

Objective: The objective of the Balloon Pop Challenge is to promote teamwork and coordination among participants.

Age Group: Suitable for youth aged 10 and above.

Number of Participants: Can be played with any number of participants, ideally in teams of 4-6.

Materials Required/Setting: Balloons and a large open space, such as a gymnasium or outdoor field.

Timing: The game typically lasts for 10-15 minutes, depending on the number of rounds played.

How to Conduct: Divide participants into teams and give each team a balloon. Instruct the teams to keep the balloon in the air for as long as possible without using their hands. They can use any other part of their body to keep the balloon aloft. The team that keeps their balloon in the air the longest wins.

Trainer Observations: Observe how well the teams communicate and work together to keep the balloon in the air. Note any strategies they use and how effective they are.

Prompting Discussion: After the game, discuss with the participants the importance of teamwork and coordination in achieving a common goal. Ask them to reflect on how they communicated with their teammates and what they could do differently next time.

Application/Learning: The Balloon Pop Challenge teaches participants the value of teamwork, communication, and coordination. It also highlights the importance of perseverance and adaptability when faced with challenges.

2. Silly String Tag

Objective: The objective of Silly String Tag is to encourage physical activity and laughter among participants.

Age Group: Suitable for youth aged 8 and above.

Number of Participants: Can be played with any number of participants, but works best with larger groups.

Materials Required/Setting: Silly string cans and an open outdoor space where participants can move freely.

Timing: The game typically lasts for 15-20 minutes, depending on the size of the playing area and the number of participants.

How to Conduct: Choose one person to be "it." Instead of tagging other players with their hands, the person who is "it" must tag others by spraying them with silly string. Once a player is tagged, they become "it" and the game continues.

Trainer Observations: Observe how participants move and react to being sprayed with silly string. Note any instances of creativity or humor.

Prompting Discussion: After the game, discuss with the participants how they felt while playing and how laughter can be a great way to relieve stress and bond with others.

Application/Learning: Silly String Tag teaches participants the importance of staying active and having fun, even in simple and silly ways. It also shows how laughter can improve mood and create a positive atmosphere.

3. Musical Chairs Remix

Objective: The objective of Musical Chairs Remix is to add a twist to the classic game of musical chairs, encouraging participants to perform dance moves instead of sitting.

Age Group: Suitable for youth aged 6 and above.

Number of Participants: Can be played with any number of participants, but works best with larger groups.

Materials Required/Setting: Chairs and music. Set up the chairs in a circle with enough space for participants to dance around them.

Timing: The game typically lasts for 10-15 minutes, depending on the number of rounds played and the speed of the music.

How to Conduct: Start the music and have participants dance around the chairs. When the music stops, they must perform a dance move instead of sitting in a chair. Remove one chair each round until only one chair remains, and the last person standing wins.

Trainer Observations: Observe how participants interpret the dance moves and how they interact with each other during the game.

Prompting Discussion: After the game, discuss with the participants how adding a twist to a classic game can make it more fun and challenging. Ask them to share their favorite dance moves from the game.

Application/Learning: Musical Chairs Remix encourages participants to think creatively and adapt to new challenges. It also promotes physical activity and coordination.

4. Emoji Charades

Objective: The objective of Emoji Charades is to encourage creativity and expression among participants.

Age Group: Suitable for youth aged 8 and above.

Number of Participants: Can be played with any number of participants, but works best with smaller groups.

Materials Required/Setting: Emoji cards or pictures of emojis.

Timing: The game typically lasts for 15-20 minutes, depending on the number of rounds played and the difficulty of the emojis.

How to Conduct: Divide participants into teams. One participant from each team selects an emoji card and must act out the emotion or action represented by the emoji while the rest of the team guesses.

Trainer Observations: Observe how participants interpret the emojis and how they express the emotions or actions.

Prompting Discussion: After the game, discuss with the participants how emojis are used to convey emotions and how body language can also communicate feelings.

Application/Learning: Emoji Charades helps participants explore different ways of expressing themselves and encourages empathy and understanding of others' emotions.

5. Obstacle Course Challenge

Objective: The objective of the Obstacle Course Challenge is to promote physical activity and teamwork among participants.

Age Group: Suitable for youth aged 10 and above.

Number of Participants: Can be played with any number of participants, but works best with teams of 4-6.

Materials Required/Setting: Various obstacles such as cones, ropes, and tires set up in a large outdoor space.

Timing: The game typically lasts for 20-30 minutes, depending on the complexity of the course and the number of teams.

How to Conduct: Set up an obstacle course with various challenges such as crawling under ropes, jumping over tires, and weaving between cones. Time each team as they navigate through the course, and the team with the fastest time wins.

Trainer Observations: Observe how teams communicate and work together to overcome the obstacles. Note any instances of leadership or problem-solving skills.

Prompting Discussion: After the game, discuss with the participants how they worked together as a team to complete the course. Ask them to reflect on the challenges they faced and how they overcame them.

Application/Learning: The Obstacle Course Challenge teaches participants the value of teamwork, perseverance, and physical fitness. It also highlights the importance of communication and cooperation in achieving a common goal.

6. Glow Stick Dance Party

Objective: The objective of the Glow Stick Dance Party is to create a fun and energetic atmosphere for participants.

Age Group: Suitable for youth aged 12 and above.

Number of Participants: Can be played with any number of participants, ideally in a group setting.

Materials Required/Setting: Glow sticks and music. The game is best played in a darkened room or outdoor area with enough space for dancing.

Timing: The party typically lasts for 30-45 minutes, depending on the energy level of the participants and the length of the music playlist.

How to Conduct: Distribute glow sticks to all participants and start playing upbeat music. Encourage participants to dance and move freely around the space, using the glow sticks to create colorful patterns and effects. You can also add fun challenges or dance-off competitions to keep the energy high.

Trainer Observations: Observe how participants interact with each other and express themselves through dance. Note any creative or unique dance moves.

Prompting Discussion: After the dance party, discuss with the participants how music and dance can be used to uplift moods and create a positive atmosphere. Ask them to share their favorite moments from the party.

Application/Learning: The Glow Stick Dance Party helps participants let loose and have fun while also promoting physical activity and creativity. It can also be a great way to relieve stress and improve mood.

7. Human Knot

Objective: The objective of the Human Knot game is to promote teamwork and problem-solving skills among participants.

Age Group: Suitable for youth aged 10 and above.

Number of Participants: Best played with a group of 8-20 participants.

Materials Required/Setting: None. The game can be played indoors or outdoors in an open space.

Timing: The game typically lasts for 10-15 minutes, depending on the complexity of the knot.

How to Conduct: Participants stand in a circle and reach in to grab hands with two different people across from them, creating a "human knot." Without letting go of hands, the group must work together to untangle the knot and form a circle again.

Trainer Observations: Observe how participants communicate and collaborate to solve the puzzle. Note any leadership or problem-solving skills that emerge.

Prompting Discussion: After the game, discuss with the participants how they approached the challenge and what strategies were most effective. Ask them to reflect on the importance of teamwork and communication in solving problems.

Application/Learning: The Human Knot game teaches participants the value of working together towards a common goal and the importance of clear communication and cooperation.

8. Story Circle

Objective: The objective of the Story Circle game is to encourage creativity and storytelling among participants.

Age Group: Suitable for youth aged 8 and above.

Number of Participants: Can be played with any number of participants, but works best with smaller groups of 6-10.

Materials Required/Setting: None. The game can be played indoors or outdoors in a comfortable sitting area.

Timing: The game typically lasts for 20-30 minutes, depending on the length of the story.

How to Conduct: Participants sit in a circle and take turns adding a sentence to create a collaborative story. Each person continues the story from where the previous person left off, building on the plot and characters as they go.

Trainer Observations: Observe how participants contribute to the story and how they build on each other's ideas. Note any creative twists or memorable moments in the storytelling.

Prompting Discussion: After the game, discuss with the participants how they worked together to create a story and how they felt about the final outcome. Ask them to reflect on the importance of imagination and creativity in storytelling.

Application/Learning: The Story Circle game helps participants develop their storytelling skills and encourages them to think creatively. It also fosters a sense of collaboration and shared ownership of the narrative.

9. Hula Hoop Challenge

Objective: The objective of the Hula Hoop Challenge is to improve coordination and have fun.

Age Group: Suitable for youth aged 6 and above.

Number of Participants: Can be played with any number of participants, ideally in a group setting.

Materials Required/Setting: Hula hoops. The game is best played in an open outdoor area with enough space for participants to move freely.

Timing: The challenge typically lasts for 10-15 minutes, depending on the number of rounds played.

How to Conduct: Participants compete to see who can keep a hula hoop spinning around their waist the longest. You can also add fun challenges, such as spinning the hoop on different body parts or moving while hooping.

Trainer Observations: Observe how participants master the technique of hula hooping and how they react to the challenge. Note any strategies or tips they share with each other.

Prompting Discussion: After the challenge, discuss with the participants how they improved their hula hooping skills and what techniques worked best for them. Ask them to reflect on the importance of practice and perseverance in mastering a new skill.

Application/Learning: The Hula Hoop Challenge helps participants improve their coordination and balance while also promoting friendly competition and teamwork.

10. Water Balloon Toss

Objective: The objective of the Water Balloon Toss is to cool off and have fun.

Age Group: Suitable for youth aged 8 and above.

Number of Participants: Can be played with pairs of participants, but works best with larger groups divided into teams.

Materials Required/Setting: Water balloons. The game is best played outdoors in a grassy area.

Timing: The game typically lasts for 15-20 minutes, depending on the number of balloons and the size of the playing area.

How to Conduct: Participants toss water balloons to each other, taking a step back after each successful catch. The team that can toss the balloon the farthest distance without breaking it wins.

Trainer Observations: Observe how participants handle the water balloons and how they interact with their teammates. Note any instances of teamwork or sportsmanship.

Prompting Discussion: After the game, discuss with the participants how they stayed cool and had fun during the activity. Ask them to reflect on the importance of staying active and hydrated during outdoor play.

Application/Learning: The Water Balloon Toss teaches participants the importance of teamwork and coordination while also providing a fun way to cool off on a hot day.

11. Paper Plane Race

Objective: The objective of the Paper Plane Race is to encourage creativity and competition among participants.

Age Group: Suitable for youth aged 8 and above.

Number of Participants: Can be played with any number of participants, ideally in pairs or small groups.

Materials Required/Setting: Paper and markers. The game can be played indoors or outdoors in a space with enough room for flying paper planes.

Timing: The race typically lasts for 10-15 minutes, depending on the complexity of the course and the number of participants.

How to Conduct: Provide each participant with a sheet of paper and markers. Instruct them to fold and decorate their paper planes however they like. Once everyone has created their planes, designate a start and finish line for the race. Participants then launch their planes and race them to the finish line. The first plane to cross the finish line wins.

Trainer Observations: Observe how participants design their paper planes and how they interact with each other during the race. Note any strategies or techniques they use to improve the performance of their planes.

Prompting Discussion: After the race, discuss with the participants how they came up with their plane designs and what they learned from the experience. Ask them to reflect on the importance of creativity and experimentation in problem-solving.

Application/Learning: The Paper Plane Race teaches participants the value of creativity and innovation in achieving their goals. It also promotes friendly competition and sportsmanship.

12. Animal Charades

Objective: The objective of Animal Charades is to promote creativity and movement among participants.

Age Group: Suitable for youth aged 6 and above.

Number of Participants: Can be played with any number of participants, ideally in small groups.

Materials Required/Setting: Animal cards with names or pictures of animals. The game can be played indoors or outdoors in a space with enough room for movement.

Timing: The game typically lasts for 15-20 minutes, depending on the number of rounds played.

How to Conduct: Divide participants into teams. One person from each team selects an animal card without showing it to the others. They then act out the movements and sounds of that animal while the rest of the team guesses the animal. The team that guesses correctly earns a point.

Trainer Observations: Observe how participants mimic the movements and sounds of the animals. Note any creativity or humor in their performances.

Prompting Discussion: After the game, discuss with the participants how they approached acting out the animals and what strategies were most effective. Ask them to reflect on the importance of body language and expression in communication.

Application/Learning: Animal Charades helps participants develop their creativity and imagination while also encouraging them to be active and expressive.

13. Back-to-Back Drawing

Objective: The objective of Back-to-Back Drawing is to improve communication and teamwork among participants.

Age Group: Suitable for youth aged 10 and above.

Number of Participants: Best played in pairs.

Materials Required/Setting: Paper and markers. The game can be played indoors or outdoors in a comfortable sitting area.

Timing: The game typically lasts for 10-15 minutes, depending on the complexity of the drawings.

How to Conduct: Pair participants up and have them sit back-to-back. One person describes a simple picture to their partner, who then tries to draw it based on the description alone. After a set amount of time, the pairs compare the original picture with the drawing to see how well they communicated.

Trainer Observations: Observe how well the pairs communicate and how accurately the drawings represent the original pictures. Note any challenges or successes in the communication process.

Prompting Discussion: After the game, discuss with the participants the importance of clear and concise communication. Ask them to reflect on how they could improve their communication skills in everyday interactions.

Application/Learning: Back-to-Back Drawing helps participants understand the importance of effective communication and listening skills in working together towards a common goal.

14. Word Association Game

Objective: The objective of the Word Association Game is to stimulate creativity and quick thinking among participants.

Age Group: Suitable for youth aged 12 and above.

Number of Participants: Can be played with any number of participants, ideally in a group setting.

Materials Required/Setting: None. The game can be played indoors or outdoors in a comfortable sitting area.

Timing: The game typically lasts for 10-15 minutes, depending on the number of rounds played.

How to Conduct: Start with a random word, and then each participant says a word related to the previous word, forming a chain of associations. For example, if the starting word is "tree," the next word could be "leaves," then "fall," and so on.

Trainer Observations: Observe how quickly participants respond and the variety of words they come up with. Note any patterns or themes in their associations.

Prompting Discussion: After the game, discuss with the participants how they approached making word associations and what strategies helped them come up with ideas. Ask them to reflect on the importance of creativity and flexibility in thinking.

Application/Learning: The Word Association Game helps participants think quickly and creatively, improving their ability to make connections and think outside the box.

15. Sponge Relay

Objective: The objective of the Sponge Relay is to have fun and cool off.

Age Group: Suitable for youth aged 8 and above.

Number of Participants: Best played with teams of 4-6 participants.

Materials Required/Setting: Sponges and buckets of water. The game is best played outdoors in a grassy area.

Timing: The relay typically lasts for 15-20 minutes, depending on the size of the teams and the distance of the relay.

How to Conduct: Divide participants into teams and set up a relay course with a starting line and a bucket of water at the other end. The first player in each team soaks a sponge in the water, then runs to the other end of the course and squeezes the water into a bucket. They then run back and tag the next player, who repeats the process. The team that fills their bucket first wins.

Trainer Observations: Observe how teams strategize and communicate during the relay. Note any instances of teamwork or leadership.

Prompting Discussion: After the relay, discuss with the participants how they worked together as a team to complete the relay. Ask them to reflect on the importance of cooperation and coordination in achieving a common goal.

Application/Learning: The Sponge Relay teaches participants the value of teamwork and cooperation while also providing a fun way to stay active and cool off.

16. Scavenger Hunt

Objective: The objective of the Scavenger Hunt is to promote teamwork and problem-solving skills among participants.

Age Group: Suitable for youth aged 10 and above.

Number of Participants: Can be played with any number of participants, ideally in teams of 3-5.

Materials Required/Setting: A list of items to find and bags to collect them in. The game can be played indoors or outdoors in a space with enough room to hide items.

Timing: The scavenger hunt typically lasts for 30-45 minutes, depending on the number of items and the size of the playing area.

How to Conduct: Divide participants into teams and give each team a list of items to find. The teams must work together to locate and collect the items within a specified time limit. The team that finds the most items wins.

Trainer Observations: Observe how teams communicate and collaborate to find the items. Note any strategies or leadership skills that emerge.

Prompting Discussion: After the scavenger hunt, discuss with the participants how they approached finding the items and what challenges they faced. Ask them to reflect on the importance of teamwork and communication in achieving a common goal.

Application/Learning: The Scavenger Hunt helps participants develop their problem-solving skills and promotes teamwork and cooperation.

17. Mystery Box

Objective: The objective of the Mystery Box game is to stimulate curiosity and creativity among participants.

Age Group: Suitable for youth aged 8 and above.

Number of Participants: Can be played with any number of participants, ideally in pairs or small groups.

Materials Required/Setting: A box filled with mystery items. The game can be played indoors or outdoors in a comfortable sitting area.

Timing: The game typically lasts for 15-20 minutes, depending on the number of rounds played.

How to Conduct: Fill a box with various mystery items, such as household objects, toys, or natural items. Participants take turns reaching into the box and feeling the mystery items without looking. They then try to guess what each item is based on touch alone.

Trainer Observations: Observe how participants use their sense of touch to guess the mystery items. Note any creative or imaginative guesses.

Prompting Discussion: After the game, discuss with the participants how they approached guessing the mystery items and what strategies were most effective. Ask them to reflect on the importance of curiosity and exploration in learning.

Application/Learning: The Mystery Box game encourages participants to use their senses and think creatively, fostering a sense of curiosity and wonder.

18. Dance Off

Objective: The objective of the Dance Off is to encourage creativity and movement among participants.

Age Group: Suitable for youth aged 6 and above.

Number of Participants: Can be played with any number of participants, ideally in a group setting.

Materials Required/Setting: Music. The game can be played indoors or outdoors in a space with enough room for dancing.

Timing: The Dance Off typically lasts for 20-30 minutes, depending on the number of participants and the length of the music playlist.

How to Conduct: Play upbeat music and invite participants to take turns showcasing their best dance moves. Encourage creativity and individuality in their performances.

Trainer Observations: Observe how participants express themselves through dance and how they interact with the music. Note any unique or creative dance moves.

Prompting Discussion: After the Dance Off, discuss with the participants how they felt while dancing and what inspired their dance moves. Ask them to reflect on the importance of self-expression and creativity in life.

Application/Learning: The Dance Off helps participants feel more comfortable expressing themselves through movement and encourages them to explore their creativity.

19. Minute to Win It Challenges

Objective: The objective of Minute to Win It Challenges is to add excitement and competition to the game.

Age Group: Suitable for youth aged 10 and above.

Number of Participants: Can be played with any number of participants, ideally in a group setting.

Materials Required/Setting: Various household items for the challenges. The game can be played indoors or outdoors in a space with enough room for the challenges.

Timing: Each challenge lasts for 1 minute, with multiple challenges played in a row.

How to Conduct: Set up a series of short challenges using everyday items, such as stacking cups or moving cookies from the forehead to the mouth. Participants compete against each other to complete the challenges in under a minute.

Trainer Observations: Observe how participants strategize and perform under pressure during the challenges. Note any teamwork or leadership skills that emerge.

Prompting Discussion: After the challenges, discuss with the participants how they approached each challenge and what techniques were most effective. Ask them to reflect on the importance of perseverance and quick thinking in overcoming challenges.

Application/Learning: Minute to Win It Challenges help participants develop their problem-solving skills and ability to perform under pressure, all while having fun and competing with their peers.

20. Fruit Ninja

Objective: The objective of the Fruit Ninja game is to promote physical activity and coordination among participants.

Age Group: Suitable for youth aged 8 and above.

Number of Participants: Can be played with any number of participants, ideally in pairs or small groups.

Materials Required/Setting: Balloons and toy swords. The game can be played outdoors in a safe area with enough room to swing the toy swords.

Timing: The game typically lasts for 10-15 minutes, depending on the number of balloons and the size of the playing area.

How to Conduct: Inflate several balloons and scatter them around the playing area. Participants use toy swords to pop the balloons, mimicking the game "Fruit Ninja."

Trainer Observations: Observe how participants use their toy swords to pop the balloons and how they move around the playing area. Note any creative or effective techniques they use.

Prompting Discussion: After the game, discuss with the participants how they approached popping the balloons and what strategies worked best for them. Ask them to reflect on the importance of physical activity and coordination in staying healthy.

Application/Learning: Fruit Ninja helps participants improve their coordination and reflexes while also providing a fun and active way to play.

21. Capture the Flag

Objective: The objective of Capture the Flag is to encourage teamwork and strategy among participants.

Age Group: Suitable for youth aged 10 and above.

Number of Participants: Can be played with any number of participants, ideally in teams of 4-8.

Materials Required/Setting: Flags for each team, boundaries to mark the playing area. The game is typically played outdoors in a large, open space.

Timing: The game typically lasts for 30-45 minutes, depending on the size of the playing area and the number of participants.

How to Conduct: Divide participants into two teams and designate a flag for each team. Each team must hide their flag somewhere in their territory. The objective is to capture the other team's flag and bring it back to their own territory without being tagged by opponents. If a player is tagged, they are sent to "jail" and can only be freed if a teammate tags them.

Trainer Observations: Observe how teams strategize and communicate during the game. Note any instances of teamwork or leadership.

Prompting Discussion: After the game, discuss with the participants the strategies they used and what they learned about teamwork and strategy. Ask them to reflect on how they can apply these skills in other areas of their lives.

Application/Learning: Capture the Flag helps participants develop their teamwork and strategic thinking skills while also providing a fun and active way to play.

22. Marshmallow Tower

Objective: The objective of the Marshmallow Tower game is to promote teamwork and problem-solving skills among participants.

Age Group: Suitable for youth aged 8 and above.

Number of Participants: Can be played with any number of participants, ideally in teams of 3-5.

Materials Required/Setting: Marshmallows, spaghetti noodles, tape. The game can be played indoors on a flat surface.

Timing: The game typically lasts for 20-30 minutes, depending on the complexity of the towers and the number of teams.

How to Conduct: Divide participants into teams and provide each team with marshmallows, spaghetti noodles, and tape. The teams must work together to build the tallest tower using only these materials. The tower must be able to stand on its own for at least 10 seconds.

Trainer Observations: Observe how teams collaborate and communicate during the tower-building process. Note any creative solutions or leadership skills that emerge.

Prompting Discussion: After the game, discuss with the participants the challenges they faced and how they overcame them. Ask them to reflect on the importance of teamwork and creative thinking in solving problems.

Application/Learning: The Marshmallow Tower game helps participants develop their teamwork and problem-solving skills while also fostering creativity and innovation.

23. Guess the Sound

Objective: The objective of Guess the Sound is to stimulate listening skills and creativity among participants.

Age Group: Suitable for youth aged 6 and above.

Number of Participants: Can be played with any number of participants, ideally in a group setting.

Materials Required/Setting: Various noise-making objects, such as bells, whistles, or musical instruments. The game can be played indoors or outdoors in a quiet space.

Timing: The game typically lasts for 10-15 minutes, depending on the number of sounds played.

How to Conduct: Play various sounds for the participants, such as animal noises, musical instruments, or everyday sounds. Participants must guess what is making the noise. The person who guesses correctly earns a point.

Trainer Observations: Observe how participants listen and react to the sounds. Note any creative or unique guesses.

Prompting Discussion: After the game, discuss with the participants the sounds they heard and how they approached guessing the sources of the sounds. Ask them to reflect on the importance of listening skills in everyday life.

Application/Learning: Guess the Sound helps participants develop their listening skills and encourages them to think creatively about the sounds they hear.

24. Freeze Dance

Objective: The objective of Freeze Dance is to encourage movement and listening skills among participants.

Age Group: Suitable for youth aged 4 and above.

Number of Participants: Can be played with any number of participants, ideally in a group setting.

Materials Required/Setting: Music. The game can be played indoors or outdoors in a space with enough room for dancing.

Timing: The game typically lasts for 10-15 minutes, depending on the length of the music playlist.

How to Conduct: Play upbeat music and invite participants to dance. When the music stops, participants must freeze in place. Anyone caught moving after the music stops is out. Play continues until only one dancer remains.

Trainer Observations: Observe how participants move and freeze in response to the music. Note any creative dance moves or interactions between participants.

Prompting Discussion: After the game, discuss with the participants how they felt while dancing and freezing. Ask them to reflect on the importance of listening and following instructions.

Application/Learning: Freeze Dance helps participants develop their listening skills and encourages them to be active and expressive through dance.

25. Pictionary

Objective: The objective of Pictionary is to stimulate creativity and teamwork among participants.

Age Group: Suitable for youth aged 8 and above.

Number of Participants: Can be played with any number of participants, ideally in teams of 2-4.

Materials Required/Setting: Paper, markers, Pictionary cards (or a list of words or phrases). The game can be played indoors on a flat surface.

Timing: The game typically lasts for 20-30 minutes, depending on the number of rounds played.

How to Conduct: Divide participants into teams. One player from each team draws a picture of a word or phrase while the rest of the team tries to guess what it is. The team that guesses correctly earns a point.

Trainer Observations: Observe how teams communicate and collaborate during the game. Note any creative drawing techniques or successful guessing strategies.

Prompting Discussion: After the game, discuss with the participants the drawings they created and how they guessed the words or phrases. Ask them to reflect on the importance of teamwork and creativity in problem-solving.

Application/Learning: Pictionary helps participants develop their creativity and communication skills while also providing a fun and interactive way to play.

26. Simon Says

Objective: The objective of Simon Says is to promote listening skills and following directions among participants.

Age Group: Suitable for youth aged 4 and above.

Number of Participants: Can be played with any number of participants, ideally in a group setting.

Materials Required/Setting: None. The game can be played indoors or outdoors in a space with enough room for movement.

Timing: The game typically lasts for 10-15 minutes, depending on the number of commands given.

How to Conduct: One person is designated as "Simon" and gives commands to the other players, such as "Simon says touch your toes." Players must only follow the commands that begin with "Simon says." If "Simon" gives a command without saying "Simon says" first, players who follow that command are out. The last player remaining wins.

Trainer Observations: Observe how participants listen and respond to the commands. Note any instances of confusion or hesitation.

Prompting Discussion: After the game, discuss with the participants the importance of listening carefully and following instructions. Ask them to reflect on times when listening skills are important in everyday life.

Application/Learning: Simon Says helps participants develop their listening skills and teaches them to pay attention to detail.

27. Bubble Wrap Stomp

Objective: The objective of Bubble Wrap Stomp is to have fun and relieve stress.

Age Group: Suitable for youth aged 6 and above.

Number of Participants: Can be played with any number of participants, ideally in a group setting.

Materials Required/Setting: Bubble wrap. The game can be played indoors on a flat surface.

Timing: The game typically lasts for 10-15 minutes, depending on the amount of bubble wrap available.

How to Conduct: Lay out a large piece of bubble wrap on the floor. Participants take turns stomping on the bubble wrap to pop the bubbles. Encourage them to have fun and make as much noise as they can.

Trainer Observations: Observe how participants express themselves while stomping on the bubble wrap. Note any signs of enjoyment or stress relief.

Prompting Discussion: After the game, discuss with the participants how they felt while stomping on the bubble wrap. Ask them to reflect on the idea of using simple activities to relieve stress.

Application/Learning: Bubble Wrap Stomp provides a fun and interactive way for participants to release tension and enjoy themselves.

28. Hot Potato

Objective: The objective of Hot Potato is to add excitement and movement to the game.

Age Group: Suitable for youth aged 4 and above.

Number of Participants: Can be played with any number of participants, ideally in a group setting.

Materials Required/Setting: Soft object, such as a ball. The game can be played indoors or outdoors in a space with enough room for movement.

Timing: The game typically lasts for 10-15 minutes, depending on the speed of the music.

How to Conduct: Participants stand in a circle and pass the soft object (the "hot potato") around while music plays. When the music stops, the person holding the hot potato is out. Play continues until only one player remains.

Trainer Observations: Observe how participants react when the music stops and they are holding the hot potato. Note any strategies they use to pass the object quickly.

Prompting Discussion: After the game, discuss with the participants the importance of being alert and responsive in fast-paced situations. Ask them to reflect on how they can apply this awareness in other areas of their lives.

Application/Learning: Hot Potato helps participants develop their reflexes and teaches them to react quickly to changing circumstances.

29. Limbo

Objective: The objective of Limbo is to encourage flexibility and have fun.

Age Group: Suitable for youth aged 6 and above.

Number of Participants: Can be played with any number of participants, ideally in a group setting.

Materials Required/Setting: Limbo stick, music. The game can be played indoors or outdoors in a space with enough room for movement.

Timing: The game typically lasts for 10-15 minutes, depending on the number of participants and the height of the limbo stick.

How to Conduct: Two people hold the limbo stick horizontally while participants take turns trying to limbo under it without touching it or falling. After each round, the limbo stick is lowered slightly. Players who touch the stick or fall are out. The last player remaining wins.

Trainer Observations: Observe how participants bend and move to limbo under the stick. Note any signs of flexibility or agility.

Prompting Discussion: After the game, discuss with the participants the importance of staying active and flexible. Ask them to reflect on how they can incorporate more movement into their daily routines.

Application/Learning: Limbo helps participants improve their flexibility and balance while also providing a fun and engaging way to play.

30. Sock Puppet Theater

Objective: The objective of Sock Puppet Theater is to stimulate creativity and imagination among participants.

Age Group: Suitable for youth aged 8 and above.

Number of Participants: Can be played with any number of participants, ideally in pairs or small groups.

Materials Required/Setting: Socks, markers, craft supplies. The game can be played indoors on a table or makeshift stage.

Timing: The game typically lasts for 20-30 minutes, depending on the length of the puppet shows.

How to Conduct: Participants create sock puppets using socks and craft supplies. They then use their puppets to perform short puppet shows, either improvising or following a script.

Trainer Observations: Observe how participants use their creativity to design and perform with their sock puppets. Note any unique puppet characters or storylines.

Prompting Discussion: After the game, discuss with the participants the puppet shows they created and performed. Ask them to reflect on the storytelling process and how they brought their puppet characters to life.

Application/Learning: Sock Puppet Theater helps participants develop their creativity and storytelling skills while also providing a fun and imaginative way to play.

31. Bingo

Objective: The objective of Bingo is to add a fun and competitive element to the game.

Age Group: Suitable for youth aged 6 and above.

Number of Participants: Can be played with any number of participants, ideally in a group setting.

Materials Required/Setting: Bingo cards, markers. The game can be played indoors at a table.

Timing: The game typically lasts for 20-30 minutes, depending on the speed of calling out numbers.

How to Conduct: Distribute bingo cards to each participant and provide markers. Call out numbers randomly, and participants mark their cards accordingly. The first player to complete a row, column, or diagonal shouts "Bingo!" and wins the game.

Trainer Observations: Observe how participants focus on their bingo cards and react when they are close to winning. Note any strategies they use to mark their cards quickly.

Prompting Discussion: After the game, discuss with the participants the strategies they used to play bingo. Ask them to reflect on how they can apply these strategies to other games or activities.

Application/Learning: Bingo helps participants develop their concentration and number recognition skills while also providing a fun and competitive gaming experience.

32. Paper Bag Skits

Objective: The objective of Paper Bag Skits is to encourage creativity and teamwork among participants.

Age Group: Suitable for youth aged 8 and above.

Number of Participants: Can be played with any number of participants, ideally in small groups.

Materials Required/Setting: Paper bags, random objects. The game can be played indoors in a space with enough room for movement.

Timing: The game typically lasts for 20-30 minutes, depending on the length of the skits.

How to Conduct: Divide participants into teams and provide each team with a paper bag filled with random objects. Teams must create a short skit using all the objects in the bag within a specified time limit.

Trainer Observations: Observe how participants work together to incorporate the random objects into their skits. Note any creative use of the objects.

Prompting Discussion: After the game, discuss with the participants the skits they created and the process of working together as a team. Ask them to reflect on the importance of teamwork in achieving a common goal.

Application/Learning: Paper Bag Skits help participants develop their creativity and teamwork skills while also encouraging them to think outside the box.

33. Duck Duck Goose

Objective: The objective of Duck Duck Goose is to promote movement and laughter among participants.
Age Group: Suitable for youth aged 4 and above.
Number of Participants: Can be played with any number of participants, ideally in a group setting.
Materials Required/Setting: None. The game can be played indoors or outdoors in an open space.
Timing: The game typically lasts for 10-15 minutes, depending on the speed of the players.
How to Conduct: Participants sit in a circle, and one person walks around tapping others on the head, saying "duck" until they choose someone to chase them as they say "goose." The "goose" must chase the "duck" around the circle and try to tag them before they reach the empty spot in the circle.
Trainer Observations: Observe how participants react when they are chosen as the "goose" and how they move around the circle. Note any instances of excitement or laughter.
Prompting Discussion: After the game, discuss with the participants the importance of staying active and having fun. Ask them to reflect on how physical activity can improve their mood and energy levels.
Application/Learning: Duck Duck Goose helps participants develop their social skills and promotes physical activity in a playful setting.

34. DIY Bracelets

Objective: The objective of DIY Bracelets is to encourage creativity and fine motor skills among participants.

Age Group: Suitable for youth aged 6 and above.

Number of Participants: Can be played with any number of participants, ideally in a group setting.

Materials Required/Setting: Beads, string. The game can be played indoors at a table.

Timing: The game typically lasts for 20-30 minutes, depending on the complexity of the bracelets.

How to Conduct: Provide participants with beads and string, and let them create their own bracelets. Encourage them to be creative with their designs and use different colors and patterns.

Trainer Observations: Observe how participants thread the beads onto the string and how they design their bracelets. Note any unique patterns or designs.

Prompting Discussion: After the game, discuss with the participants the bracelets they created. Ask them to reflect on the creative process and how they can express themselves through art.

Application/Learning: DIY Bracelets help participants develop their creativity and fine motor skills while also providing a fun and relaxing activity.

35. Frisbee Tic-Tac-Toe

Objective: The objective of Frisbee Tic-Tac-Toe is to combine physical activity with strategy.
Age Group: Suitable for youth aged 8 and above.
Number of Participants: Can be played with two players or two teams of any size.
Materials Required/Setting: Frisbee, tic-tac-toe grid. The game can be played outdoors on a flat surface.
Timing: The game typically lasts for 15-20 minutes, depending on the speed of the players.
How to Conduct: Draw a large tic-tac-toe grid on the ground and place markers for each player or team. Players take turns throwing a frisbee to land on a square on the grid, trying to get three in a row horizontally, vertically, or diagonally.
Trainer Observations: Observe how players strategize their throws to win the game. Note any instances of teamwork or strategic thinking.
Prompting Discussion: After the game, discuss with the participants the strategies they used to win. Ask them to reflect on how they can apply strategic thinking in other areas of their lives.
Application/Learning: Frisbee Tic-Tac-Toe helps participants develop their strategic thinking and hand-eye coordination while also providing a fun and active game.

36. Giant Jenga

Objective: The objective of Giant Jenga is to promote balance and strategy among participants.
Age Group: Suitable for youth aged 8 and above.
Number of Participants: Can be played with any number of participants, ideally in small groups.
Materials Required/Setting: Giant Jenga blocks. The game can be played indoors or outdoors on a flat surface.
Timing: The game typically lasts for 20-30 minutes, depending on the speed of the players.
How to Conduct: Build a tower using the Giant Jenga blocks. Participants take turns removing one block at a time from any level of the tower and placing it on top. The game continues until the tower collapses, and the player who made it collapse loses.
Trainer Observations: Observe how participants carefully choose blocks to remove and place, considering the balance of the tower. Note any strategies they use to prevent the tower from collapsing.
Prompting Discussion: After the game, discuss with the participants the strategies they used to play Giant Jenga. Ask them to reflect on how they can apply these strategies to other balancing activities or situations that require strategic thinking.
Application/Learning: Giant Jenga helps participants develop their balance and strategic thinking skills while also providing a fun and challenging game.

37. Blindfolded Obstacle Course

Objective: The objective of the Blindfolded Obstacle Course is to build trust and communication among participants.

Age Group: Suitable for youth aged 10 and above.

Number of Participants: Can be played with pairs of participants, one blindfolded and one guiding.

Materials Required/Setting: Blindfolds, obstacles. The game can be played indoors or outdoors in a space with obstacles.

Timing: The game typically lasts for 20-30 minutes, depending on the complexity of the course.

How to Conduct: Set up an obstacle course with various obstacles. One participant is blindfolded and guided through the course by their partner, who can only use verbal instructions to navigate them.

Trainer Observations: Observe how participants communicate and trust each other during the game. Note any instances of effective communication or teamwork.

Prompting Discussion: After the game, discuss with the participants the importance of trust and communication in achieving a common goal. Ask them to reflect on how they can apply these skills in their daily lives.

Application/Learning: The Blindfolded Obstacle Course helps participants develop their trust and communication skills while also providing a challenging and rewarding experience.

38. Shadow Puppet Show

Objective: The objective of the Shadow Puppet Show is to stimulate creativity and imagination among participants.

Age Group: Suitable for youth aged 6 and above.

Number of Participants: Can be played with any number of participants, ideally in small groups.

Materials Required/Setting: Light source, hands. The game can be played indoors against a wall or on a sheet.

Timing: The game typically lasts for 15-20 minutes, depending on the length of the show.

How to Conduct: Participants use their hands to create shapes and figures on a wall or sheet to make shadow puppets. They can tell stories or create scenes using their shadow puppets.

Trainer Observations: Observe how participants use their hands to create different shapes and figures. Note any creative or imaginative stories they tell with their shadow puppets.

Prompting Discussion: After the game, discuss with the participants the stories they created with their shadow puppets. Ask them to reflect on how they can use their creativity and imagination in other forms of storytelling.

Application/Learning: The Shadow Puppet Show helps participants develop their creativity and imagination while also providing a fun and interactive way to tell stories.

39. Bucket Ball

Objective: The objective of Bucket Ball is to improve aim and coordination among participants.

Age Group: Suitable for youth aged 8 and above.

Number of Participants: Can be played with two players or two teams of any size.

Materials Required/Setting: Buckets, balls. The game can be played outdoors in a space with enough room for throwing.

Timing: The game typically lasts for 10-15 minutes, depending on the number of buckets and balls.

How to Conduct: Place buckets at various distances and assign point values to each bucket. Participants take turns throwing balls into the buckets to score points. The player or team with the most points wins.

Trainer Observations: Observe how participants aim and throw the balls into the buckets. Note any strategies they use to improve their accuracy and coordination.

Prompting Discussion: After the game, discuss with the participants the techniques they used to throw the balls into the buckets. Ask them to reflect on how they can apply these techniques to improve their aim in other activities.

Application/Learning: Bucket Ball helps participants develop their aim and coordination skills while also providing a fun and competitive game.

40. Guess Who?

Objective: The objective of Guess Who? is to encourage observation and deduction among participants.

Age Group: Suitable for youth aged 10 and above.

Number of Participants: Can be played with any number of participants, ideally in small groups.

Materials Required/Setting: Photos or descriptions of famous people. The game can be played indoors at a table.

Timing: The game typically lasts for 15-20 minutes, depending on the number of rounds.

How to Conduct: Choose a famous person and provide participants with photos or descriptions to guess the identity of the person. Participants ask yes or no questions to narrow down the options and make their guess.

Trainer Observations: Observe how participants ask questions and make deductions based on the information provided. Note any creative or strategic thinking they use to guess the identity of the person.

Prompting Discussion: After the game, discuss with the participants the questions they asked to guess the identity of the person. Ask them to reflect on how they can improve their observation and deduction skills in other situations.

Application/Learning: Guess Who? helps participants develop their observation and deduction skills while also providing a fun and engaging game.

41. Cup Stacking

Objective: The objective of Cup Stacking is to improve coordination and speed among participants.

Age Group: Suitable for youth aged 6 and above.

Number of Participants: Can be played with any number of participants, ideally in small groups.

Materials Required/Setting: Plastic cups. The game can be played indoors or outdoors on a flat surface.

Timing: The game typically lasts for 10-15 minutes, depending on the number of cups and participants.

How to Conduct: Participants stack cups into a pyramid and then back into a single stack as quickly as possible. They can compete against each other or try to beat their own time.

Trainer Observations: Observe how participants use their hands to stack the cups and how quickly they can complete the task. Note any strategies they use to improve their speed and coordination.

Prompting Discussion: After the game, discuss with the participants the techniques they used to stack the cups quickly. Ask them to reflect on how they can apply these techniques to other activities that require coordination and speed.

Application/Learning: Cup Stacking helps participants develop their coordination and speed while also providing a fun and challenging activity.

42. Bean Bag Toss

Objective: The objective of Bean Bag Toss is to improve aim and coordination among participants.

Age Group: Suitable for youth aged 8 and above.

Number of Participants: Can be played with two players or two teams of any size.

Materials Required/Setting: Bean bags, targets. The game can be played outdoors in a space with enough room for throwing.

Timing: The game typically lasts for 10-15 minutes, depending on the number of targets and participants.

How to Conduct: Participants toss bean bags into targets to score points. The targets can be set up at various distances to increase the challenge.

Trainer Observations: Observe how participants aim and throw the bean bags. Note any techniques they use to improve their accuracy and coordination.

Prompting Discussion: After the game, discuss with the participants the strategies they used to score points in Bean Bag Toss. Ask them to reflect on how they can apply these strategies to improve their aim in other activities.

Application/Learning: Bean Bag Toss helps participants develop their aim and coordination skills while also providing a fun and competitive game.

43. Human Tic-Tac-Toe

Objective: The objective of Human Tic-Tac-Toe is to combine strategy with physical activity among participants.

Age Group: Suitable for youth aged 10 and above.

Number of Participants: Can be played with two teams of three or more players each.

Materials Required/Setting: Rope, chalk (for outdoor play). The game is typically played outdoors on a flat surface.

Timing: The game typically lasts for 15-20 minutes, depending on the speed of the players.

How to Conduct: Create a giant tic-tac-toe grid using the rope and chalk. Divide participants into two teams and have them take turns trying to get three in a row by standing in the grid.

Trainer Observations: Observe how participants strategize to win the game. Note any teamwork or communication skills they use to coordinate their moves.

Prompting Discussion: After the game, discuss with the participants the strategies they used to win Human Tic-Tac-Toe. Ask them to reflect on how they can apply these strategies to work effectively in a team.

Application/Learning: Human Tic-Tac-Toe helps participants develop their strategy and teamwork skills while also providing a fun and interactive game.

44. Balloon Stomp

Objective: The objective of Balloon Stomp is to add excitement and physical activity among participants.

Age Group: Suitable for youth aged 6 and above.

Number of Participants: Can be played with any number of participants, ideally in a large group.

Materials Required/Setting: Balloons, string. The game is typically played indoors or outdoors in a space with enough room for movement.

Timing: The game typically lasts for 10-15 minutes, depending on the number of balloons and participants.

How to Conduct: Participants tie balloons to their ankles and try to pop each other's balloons while keeping theirs intact. The last participant with their balloon intact wins.

Trainer Observations: Observe how participants move around and try to pop each other's balloons. Note any strategies they use to protect their own balloons while popping others'.

Prompting Discussion: After the game, discuss with the participants the strategies they used to protect their balloons. Ask them to reflect on how they can apply these strategies to defend their ideas or goals in real-life situations.

Application/Learning: Balloon Stomp helps participants develop their agility and reflexes while also providing a fun and energetic activity.

45. Name That Tune

Objective: The objective of Name That Tune is to stimulate memory and musical knowledge among participants.

Age Group: Suitable for youth aged 10 and above.

Number of Participants: Can be played with any number of participants, ideally in small groups.

Materials Required/Setting: Music player, song list. The game can be played indoors in a space with enough room for listening.

Timing: The game typically lasts for 15-20 minutes, depending on the number of rounds.

How to Conduct: Play short clips of songs and have participants guess the song title and artist. Participants can earn points for correct answers.

Trainer Observations: Observe how participants listen to the music and try to recall the song title and artist. Note any musical knowledge or memory skills they demonstrate.

Prompting Discussion: After the game, discuss with the participants the songs they recognized and how they were able to recall the titles and artists. Ask them to reflect on how they can improve their memory skills in other areas.

Application/Learning: Name That Tune helps participants develop their memory and musical knowledge while also providing a fun and engaging game.

46. Water Relay

Objective: The objective of Water Relay is to cool off and have fun while promoting teamwork.

Age Group: Suitable for youth aged 8 and above.

Number of Participants: Can be played with two or more teams of three or more players each.

Materials Required/Setting: Cups, buckets of water. The game is typically played outdoors in a space with enough room for running.

Timing: The game typically lasts for 10-15 minutes, depending on the distance between the water source and the bucket.

How to Conduct: Divide participants into teams. Place a bucket at one end of the playing area and a water source (e.g., a large container filled with water) at the other end. Participants take turns filling their cups with water, then running to pour it into the bucket. The team that fills the bucket to a certain level or finishes first wins.

Trainer Observations: Observe how participants work together to fill the bucket. Note any strategies they use to minimize spills and maximize efficiency.

Prompting Discussion: After the game, discuss with the participants the importance of teamwork and coordination in achieving a common goal. Ask them to reflect on how they can apply these skills in other group activities.

Application/Learning: Water Relay helps participants develop their teamwork and coordination skills while also providing a fun and refreshing activity.

47. M&M's Icebreaker

Objective: The objective of M&M's Icebreaker is to break the ice and encourage sharing among participants.

Age Group: Suitable for youth aged 10 and above.

Number of Participants: Can be played with any number of participants, ideally in small groups.

Materials Required/Setting: M&M's candies. The game can be played indoors or outdoors in a space where participants can sit comfortably.

Timing: The game typically lasts for 10-15 minutes, depending on the number of questions and participants.

How to Conduct: Pour a bag of M&M's into a bowl. Participants take turns picking an M&M from the bowl and answering a question based on the color they pick (e.g., red for favorite food, blue for dream vacation). The questions can be pre-prepared or improvised based on the group.

Trainer Observations: Observe how participants interact with each other and share information. Note any common interests or experiences that emerge during the game.

Prompting Discussion: After the game, discuss with the participants the insights they gained about each other through the questions. Ask them to reflect on how sharing personal information can help build connections with others.

Application/Learning: M&M's Icebreaker helps participants break the ice and get to know each other better while also providing a fun and interactive activity.

48. Mindful Minute

Objective: The objective of Mindful Minute is to promote mindfulness and relaxation among participants.

Age Group: Suitable for youth aged 12 and above.

Number of Participants: Can be conducted with any number of participants, ideally in a quiet and comfortable setting.

Materials Required/Setting: None. The activity can be conducted indoors or outdoors in a space where participants can sit or lie down comfortably.

Timing: The activity typically lasts for 5-10 minutes, depending on the length of the guided meditation.

How to Conduct: Lead participants through a short mindfulness exercise, focusing on their breath or senses. Encourage them to relax and let go of any distractions or thoughts.

Trainer Observations: Observe how participants respond to the mindfulness exercise. Note any changes in their body language or demeanor.

Prompting Discussion: After the activity, discuss with the participants their experience of mindfulness. Ask them to reflect on how they can incorporate mindfulness into their daily lives to reduce stress and improve focus.

Application/Learning: Mindful Minute helps participants experience the benefits of mindfulness and relaxation, encouraging them to practice these techniques regularly.

49. Buddy Interviews

Objective: The objective of Buddy Interviews is to encourage communication and bonding among participants.

Age Group: Suitable for youth aged 10 and above.

Number of Participants: Can be conducted with any number of participants, ideally in pairs.

Materials Required/Setting: None. The activity can be conducted indoors or outdoors in a space where participants can sit comfortably.

Timing: The activity typically lasts for 15-20 minutes, depending on the depth of the interviews.

How to Conduct: Pair participants up and have them interview each other. Provide a list of questions or topics to guide the interviews, such as hobbies, favorite foods, and future goals. After the interviews, each participant introduces their partner to the group.

Trainer Observations: Observe how participants engage in the interviews. Note any common interests or experiences that emerge during the discussions.

Prompting Discussion: After the activity, discuss with the participants their experience of interviewing and being interviewed. Ask them to reflect on what they learned about their partner and how this activity helped them connect.

Application/Learning: Buddy Interviews help participants practice their communication skills and learn more about their peers, fostering a sense of connection and understanding.

50. Memory Game

Objective: The objective of the Memory Game is to stimulate memory and focus among participants.

Age Group: Suitable for youth aged 8 and above.

Number of Participants: Can be played with any number of participants, ideally in small groups.

Materials Required/Setting: Cards or pictures. The game can be played indoors or outdoors in a space where participants can sit comfortably.

Timing: The game typically lasts for 10-15 minutes, depending on the number of cards and participants.

How to Conduct: Show participants a set of cards or pictures for a short time, then have them recall as many details as possible. Participants can take turns revealing the cards or pictures to each other.

Trainer Observations: Observe how participants use their memory and focus to recall the details of the cards or pictures. Note any strategies they use to improve their memory.

Prompting Discussion: After the game, discuss with the participants their strategies for remembering the details. Ask them to reflect on how they can apply these strategies to improve their memory in other areas, such as studying or learning new skills.

Application/Learning: The Memory Game helps participants exercise their memory and focus while also providing a fun and challenging activity.

Some Ice-Breakers

1. Name Game

Objective: To help participants learn each other's names.

Age Group: Youth.

Number of Participants: Any group size.

Materials Required/Setting: None.

Timing: 10-15 minutes.

How to Conduct: Have participants stand in a circle. The first person says their name and an adjective that starts with the same letter as their name (e.g., "Funny Fred"). The next person repeats the first person's name and adjective, then adds their own. Continue around the circle until everyone has been introduced.

Trainer Observations: Observe how participants interact and remember each other's names.

Prompting Discussion: Ask participants how they felt about remembering everyone's names. Discuss the importance of remembering names in building relationships.

Application/Learning: Encourage participants to use each other's names throughout the session to reinforce learning and connection.

2. Two Truths and a Lie

Objective: To break the ice and get to know each other better.
Age Group: Youth.
Number of Participants: Any group size.
Materials Required/Setting: None.
Timing: 15-20 minutes.
How to Conduct: Each participant says three statements about themselves: two truths and one lie. The group tries to guess which statement is the lie.
Trainer Observations: Observe how participants share personal information and interact with each other.
Prompting Discussion: Discuss the importance of honesty and openness in building trust and relationships.
Application/Learning: Encourage participants to continue sharing truths about themselves to deepen connections with others.

3. Human Bingo

Objective: To encourage interaction and learning about others.

Age Group: Youth.

Number of Participants: Any group size.

Materials Required/Setting: Bingo cards with different characteristics or experiences (e.g., has traveled to another country, plays a musical instrument).

Timing: 20-30 minutes.

How to Conduct: Distribute bingo cards to each participant. Participants mingle and find others who fit the descriptions on their bingo cards. The first person to fill their bingo card wins.

Trainer Observations: Observe how participants engage with each other and discover commonalities.

Prompting Discussion: Discuss the similarities and differences among the group members. Encourage participants to share interesting facts they learned about each other.

Application/Learning: Encourage participants to continue getting to know each other beyond the game to build lasting relationships.

4. The Great Egg Drop

Objective: To promote teamwork and creativity.
Age Group: Youth.
Number of Participants: Small groups of 4-6.
Materials Required/Setting: Eggs, straws, tape, paper, and other materials for building a protective device.
Timing: 30-45 minutes.
How to Conduct: In small groups, participants design and build a contraption using the materials provided to protect an egg from breaking when dropped from a height. After building, each group drops their contraption and egg, and the one with the intact egg wins.
Trainer Observations: Observe how groups collaborate, communicate, and problem-solve.
Prompting Discussion: Discuss the challenges faced during the activity and how the groups overcame them. Highlight the importance of teamwork and creativity.
Application/Learning: Encourage participants to apply the lessons learned from the activity to real-life challenges, emphasizing the value of teamwork and innovative thinking.

5. Group Juggle

Objective: To improve coordination and teamwork.
Age Group: Youth.
Number of Participants: Any group size.
Materials Required/Setting: Soft object (e.g., ball).
Timing: 15-20 minutes.
How to Conduct: Participants stand in a circle. The facilitator starts by tossing the ball to someone across the circle, saying their name. The person who catches it then tosses it to another person, saying their name, and so on. The goal is to keep the ball moving without dropping it.
Trainer Observations: Observe how participants coordinate their movements and communicate with each other.
Prompting Discussion: Discuss the importance of clear communication and coordination in achieving a common goal.
Application/Learning: Encourage participants to apply the skills learned from the activity to improve teamwork in other settings, such as school projects or sports teams.

6. Quick Draw

Objective: To stimulate creativity and imagination.
Age Group: Youth.
Number of Participants: Any group size.
Materials Required/Setting: Paper, markers.
Timing: 10-15 minutes.
How to Conduct: Participants are given a prompt (e.g., "draw your favorite animal") and a limited time to draw their response. They then share their drawings with the group.
Trainer Observations: Observe how participants interpret and represent the prompt in their drawings.
Prompting Discussion: Discuss the different interpretations of the same prompt and how creativity can be expressed in various forms.
Application/Learning: Encourage participants to think creatively and outside the box in problem-solving and decision-making.

7. Would You Rather?

Objective: To prompt conversation and reveal preferences.

Age Group: Youth.

Number of Participants: Any group size.

Materials Required/Setting: None.

Timing: 15-20 minutes.

How to Conduct: Participants take turns asking each other "Would you rather" questions (e.g., Would you rather have the ability to fly or be invisible?).

Trainer Observations: Observe how participants consider and explain their choices.

Prompting Discussion: Discuss how people make decisions and the factors that influence their choices.

Application/Learning: Encourage participants to consider different perspectives when making decisions.

8. The Great Wind Blows

Objective: To encourage movement and quick thinking.
Age Group: Youth.
Number of Participants: Any group size.
Materials Required/Setting: None.
Timing: 10-15 minutes.
How to Conduct: Participants sit in a circle, with one person in the middle. The person in the middle says, "The great wind blows for anyone who..." followed by a statement (e.g., "The great wind blows for anyone who has a pet"). Anyone to whom the statement applies must stand up and find a new seat.
Trainer Observations: Observe how participants listen and react quickly to the statements.
Prompting Discussion: Discuss the importance of active listening and being open to new experiences.
Application/Learning: Encourage participants to be attentive and responsive in different situations.

9. Story Starters

Objective: To stimulate creativity and storytelling.
Age Group: Youth.
Number of Participants: Any group size.
Materials Required/Setting: None.
Timing: 15-20 minutes.
How to Conduct: Each participant starts a story with a sentence or phrase. The next person continues the story, and so on, building a collaborative narrative.
Trainer Observations: Observe how participants contribute to the story and build on each other's ideas.
Prompting Discussion: Discuss the elements of a good story and how storytelling can be used to convey messages effectively.
Application/Learning: Encourage participants to use their storytelling skills in creative projects and presentations.

10. The Memory Jar

Objective: To share memories and build connections.

Age Group: Youth.

Number of Participants: Any group size.

Materials Required/Setting: Jar, slips of paper.

Timing: 20-30 minutes.

How to Conduct: Each participant writes down a memorable moment on a slip of paper and puts it in the jar. The group takes turns drawing slips and sharing the memories.

Trainer Observations: Observe how participants recall and share meaningful experiences.

Prompting Discussion: Discuss the importance of creating and cherishing memories.

Application/Learning: Encourage participants to create more meaningful experiences and memories in their lives.

11. Celebrity Interview

Objective: To promote creativity and imagination.
Age Group: Youth.
Number of Participants: Any group size.
Materials Required/Setting: None.
Timing: 15-20 minutes.
How to Conduct: Each participant pretends to be a celebrity and is interviewed by the group. Others ask questions and the "celebrity" responds in character.
Trainer Observations: Observe how participants embody the characteristics of different celebrities.
Prompting Discussion: Discuss how people perceive and portray celebrities in the media.
Application/Learning: Encourage participants to explore different roles and perspectives.

12. Compliment Circle

Objective: To promote positivity and self-esteem.
Age Group: Youth.
Number of Participants: Any group size.
Materials Required/Setting: None.
Timing: 10-15 minutes.
How to Conduct: Participants sit in a circle. Each person gives a genuine compliment to the person on their right.
Trainer Observations: Observe how participants express appreciation and receive compliments.
Prompting Discussion: Discuss the impact of positive feedback on individuals and relationships.
Application/Learning: Encourage participants to practice giving and receiving compliments in their daily interactions.

Creating Your Own Energizers, Games & Activities

While this book provides a wealth of ideas for energizers, games, and activities, there may be times when you want to create your own. This chapter explores how you can develop custom activities tailored to the needs and interests of your group.

- ✓ **Identifying Objectives:** Start by identifying the specific objectives you want to achieve with the activity. Are you aiming to build teamwork, improve communication, or enhance creativity? Clearly defining your objectives will guide the design of your activity.
- ✓ **Choosing the Format:** Consider the format of your activity. Will it be a physical game, a role-playing exercise, or a discussion-based activity? Choose a format that aligns with your objectives and the preferences of your group.
- ✓ **Designing the Activity:** Create a step-by-step plan for your activity, including how it will be introduced, the rules, how it will be conducted, and how it will be concluded. Consider factors such as timing, materials needed, and any safety considerations.
- ✓ **Testing and Refining:** Before implementing your activity, test it out to ensure it achieves your objectives and is engaging for participants. Based on feedback, refine the activity as needed to improve its effectiveness.
- ✓ **Implementing the Activity:** When implementing your activity, be sure to clearly explain the rules and objectives to

participants. Encourage active participation and provide feedback and guidance as needed.
- ✓ *Reflecting and Iterating*: After the activity, take time to reflect on its effectiveness. Did it achieve your objectives? What could be improved? Use this feedback to iterate and improve your activity for future use.

Creating your own energizers, games, and activities can be a rewarding experience that allows you to tailor your efforts to the specific needs and interests of your group. Experiment, be creative, and most importantly, have fun!

Taking it Forward!

Now that you have a repertoire of energizers, games, and activities at your disposal, it's time to take your youth engagement efforts to the next level. This chapter explores how you can build on the experiences and lessons learned from these activities to create lasting impact and meaningful change.

- ✓ **Reflecting on the Experience:** After each activity, take some time to reflect on the experience with your group. Ask questions such as: What did we learn from this activity? How did it make us feel? What challenges did we face, and how did we overcome them? Reflecting on these questions can help participants internalize the lessons and insights gained from the activity.
- ✓ **Setting Goals:** Based on the insights gained from the activities, work with your group to set goals for personal or group development. These goals could be related to improving communication skills, building teamwork, or developing leadership abilities. Encourage participants to take ownership of their goals and commit to achieving them.
- ✓ **Action Plans:** Create action plans to help participants work towards their goals. These plans should include specific, measurable, achievable, relevant, and time-bound (SMART) steps. For example, if the goal is to improve communication skills, the action plan might include activities such as practicing

active listening or participating in group discussions.

✓ **Celebrating Success:** Acknowledge and celebrate the achievements of individuals and the group as a whole. This could be done through verbal praise, certificates, or other forms of recognition. Celebrating success reinforces positive behavior and encourages continued growth.

About the Author
'GERARD ASSEY'

Gerard Assey is a Graduate in Economics, a PGD in Management (HRD) and holds a Doctorate in Leadership. Gerard holds several International Qualifications in Sales, Debt Collection, Training & Teaching, and is a 'Fellow' of the prestigious 'Institute of Sales & Marketing Management'-UK, a Certified NLP Practitioner, a 'Certified Trainer', an 'Accredited Management Teacher-Behavioral Sciences', a 'Certified Competency Facilitator', a 'Certified Management Consultant'- (the International credentials of a professional management consultant, awarded in accordance with global standards of the ICMCI); and a Certification from the University of Michigan in 'Successful Negotiation: Essential Strategies and Skills'

He is also a Member of the 'National Association of Sales Professionals' backed with several years experience in varied industries, both in India and Overseas. He also holds an 'Etiquette Consultant' Certification from the USA (by Sue Fox, Author of Best Seller: 'Business Etiquette for Dummies'. She has trained some of the top celebrities' world over). He was also a recipient of a scholarship for extensive training in Japan on 'Corporate Management for India'.

Gerard Assey is 'Founder & Chief Corporate Trainer' of the Group: '**Citius, Altius, Fortius Unlimited**'- an organization that **celebrated 20 years of Glorious Service** in 2021, focusing on 3 Core Competencies:

People. Performance. Profit; in functional areas of Sales & Marketing, HR & Organizational Development, covering Recruitment, Training & Consultancy!

Having managed organizations with large Sales Forces in India & Overseas, his specialization cover extensive areas of Sales Training (All levels - Presentation, Negotiation, Key/ Strategic Accounts Management & Managerial Skills for all sectors), Bid Proposal/ Capture Planning/ Management Trainings, Retail Sales, Customer Service & Customer Retention Programs, Training for Prevention & Collection of Debt, Self & Personal Development Programs (Time Management, Teamwork & Team Building, Business Etiquette & Personal Grooming, Leadership & Managerial Skills, People Management Skills, Train-the-Trainer etc), including preparation of Custom-designed Business Manuals for Internal (HR, Induction, and Sales etc) & External use (Instruction, User Manuals).

Gerard has successfully conducted over 6100 Trainings & Workshops (as of Mar '24) all across India, Middle East, Africa, Europe & S.E. Asia. Besides public programs conducted regularly, both in India & Overseas, he has some of the top names as clients whom he services from Single Owners to large Public & Government undertakings, covering all sectors, for their in-house needs.

His website: www.CollectionSkills.com is the only one in this part of the world to be featured in the 'Collections & Credit Risk Magazine-USA' under 'Who's Who in Training' and ranks TOP, along with other websites listed below on most search engines.

Gerard is author of 119 books already (April 2024)

A few of our business related books:

1. Bite-sized Bits on Commonsense Management
2. Heart to Heart on Life's Principles'
3. How to become a Successful Manager
4. The Sales Professionals' Master Workbook of S.Y.S.T.E.M.S
5. The Professional Business Email Etiquette Handbook & Guide
6. The Professional Business Video-Conferencing Etiquette Handbook & Guide
7. Professional Presentation Skills
8. Exceptional Customer Service
9. Professional Tele-Marketing Skills
10. Professional Debt Collection Skills
11. The G.R.E.A.T. Sales & Service Workbook
12. Sales Training Advantage for Results (*The Ultimate Sales Training Manual to enable you stand out as a S.T.A.R.*)
13. CEO Daily Planner & Organizer
14. The Sales Professionals' Master Daily Planner
15. The Professional Debt Collector's Master Daily Planner
16. My Daily Planner & Organizer
17. MY EMERGENCY INFORMATION RECORD (Family Emergency & Peace of Mind Planner)
18. The Ultimate Therapist & Counselors Planner and Organizer
19. Building an Ethical Workplace
20. Managing Relationships at Work
21. Managing Business Meetings Effectively
22. Effective Delegation Skills
23. Goal Setting for Success
24. B2B Selling by Email
25. Professional Business Etiquette & Grooming
26. Dining Etiquette & Table Manners
27. Effective Networking Skills
28. Grooming, Etiquette & Manners for Teens, Young Adults & Future Leaders
29. Inter-Personal Skills
30. Get Ready, Get Hired!
31. Selling in a Recession
32. Effective Receivables Management in an Economic Downturn!
33. Real Estate & Property Sales Training

Besides regularly contributing to business & trade journals, including international ones such as the 'Creative Training Techniques' and the 'Sales News' of the U.S.A, He is also a member of several prestigious bodies & trade associations, having participated in many Conferences & Workshops in India & Overseas.

Prior to his last assignment of leading & managing a large MNC as head, Gerard had a 3-year stint in the Middle East as a Consultant with a leading British Consultancy Firm.

As the past 'Official Country Representative' for the International Business Award- 'THE STEVIES'-(the business world's own Oscar) for about 4 years- he ensured a few Indian companies that qualify for the same every year!

Gerard can be contacted at:
Email: training@Sales-Training.in,training@CollectionSkills.com
Websites:
www.Sales-Training.in
www.EtiquetteWorks.in
www.CollectionSkills.com
www.RetailSalesTraining.in
www.SalesTrainingIndia.com
www.ManualPreparation.com
www.TrainingWithPuppets.com
www.FirstContactAcademy.com
www.SalesAndMarketingRecruiter.com

Our TRAININGS that can help your team

- ✓ **Sales Effectiveness**: Selling Skills for any Sector: Service/ Logistics/ FMCG Realty/ Insurance & Finance/ Media/ SPA's, Health Clubs & Salons/ Key Account Management, Effective Negotiation Skills/ Bid & Proposal Management Skills/ Retail Sales Training: Any Sector (Auto, Jewelry, Clothing, Luxury etc)
- ✓ **Customer Service Skills**-Complaints Handling & Customer Retention
- ✓ **Debt Prevention & Collection Skills**
- ✓ **Etiquette & Grooming**
- ✓ **Leadership & Managerial Skills**
- ✓ **Self & Personal Development Skills**: Presentation Skills/ Effective Communication Skills/Business Proposal Writing Skills/ Problem Solving & Decision Making Skills/ Empowering Secretaries-The perfect PA! (For Secretaries & PA's)/ Effective Time Management/ Teamwork & Teambuilding/ P.R.I.D.E- **P**ersonal **R**esponsibility **I**n **D**elivering **E**xcellence